MW01178709

EXPRESSWAY

EXPRESSWAY

SINA QUEYRAS

COACH HOUSE BOOKS | TORONTO

Canada Council **Conseil des Arts**
for the Arts du Canada

 ONTARIO ARTS COUNCIL
CONSEIL DES ARTS DE L'ONTARIO

Published with the generous assistance of the Canada Council for
the Arts and the Ontario Arts Council. Coach House Books also
gratefully acknowledges the support of the Government of Canada
through the Book Publishing Industry Development Program.

LIBRARY AND ARCHIVES CANADA CATALOGUING IN PUBLICATION

Queyras, Sina
    Expressway / Sina Queyras.

Poems.
ISBN 978-1-55245-216-5

    I. Title.

PS8583.U3414E96 2009   c811'.6   c2009-900012-1

I

THE ENDLESS PATH OF THE NEW

'Wait now; have no rememberings of hope … '
Wallace Stevens

'If you can't see the finish line in the near
distance, don't get frustrated – turn around!
There you'll see it, miles behind you.'
Daily Horoscope, January 18, 2007

SOLITARY

1

What sympathy of sounds? What cricketing
Of concrete, what struck rubber, what society
And shifting birdsong sweetens spring's tumult?

She walks near the expressway, a patch
Of emerald turf besieged by doggy bags,
Where frolicking hounds squat to pee, crimson

Cellphone at her ear. She is calling home,
Calling the past, calling out for anyone
To hear. She is waiting, she is wanting

To be near, of flesh, of earth, on foot,
And this is her perspective: the I-95, its
Prow of condos, the Delaware's sunken

Ships and artillery shells, now *the idea* of
River, so many years since any live flesh
Could be immersed. Here the expressway

Smoothing each nuisance of wild, each terrifying
Quirk of land, uneven, forlorn paths; wanderer,
Wander, lonely as a cloud, dappled, drowned,

A melancholic pace and nowhere untouched. Nature,
One concludes, is nostalgia. Now, two hundred
Post-Romantic years – the Alps bursting into flames,

All the way to Mont Blanc, incendiary air. How far
Auschwitz? Darfur? Are we a hopeful people
Yet? She follows her uncle's gestures, paced

For lungs, each strike of stick to stone, recalls
Wordsworth's dog, the solitary path unwinds below.

What sympathy of sounds. Her father
A bag she carries in a bigger bag, lighter
Now, having scattered him across two

Provinces, up a goat path, where these
Struck peaks, a starburst of contrails, German
Songs like silt, and tiny woollen cathedrals

Whose bells mark the hours. Have we suffered enough?
Her uncle bends his century, a creeping juniper
Under which lies a tiny tin cup. *Doucement,*

Doucement, the water another source, a
Knowing (even without language) where
To drink, or how (and where) one foot

Should fall well before it does, recognition of
The stone's slice; that even rock is not solid;
Such knowledge a long-time companion rarely

Of any use other than to remind: be open, flexible,
Eye on the horizon, thumb in air for change,
Change; history with its multiple pathways.

It is not her first time here, though, in truth,
It is. But what is truth? Fact? Body? Idea?
Word? The heat waking up now, a new century

Ahead, and at the top, a bit of bread and cheese,
A cellphone out, *Ta mère*, he says,
Tell her your father is laid to rest.

3

But is anyone at rest? She traces roadways where
In occupied France her father rode his bicycle
High above the Durance, finding – as we all

Wish – a smooth path between rivets
Of the newly erected metal bridge, his hands
High above his head, or so one version

Of the legend goes. What balance, what
Lack of fear, what shock of hair, what finesse
Of foot and pout of mouth, what eloquent

Dismount, his aunts below not daring
To call out for fear of distracting he who
Like Christ could turn gravity on its head,

And for whom two sisters would devote their lives –
If not in flesh, then in suffering. What
Sympathy of sounds? Do tell me his pain

Was not in vain. Do say the bees will return,
And with them, seasons.

4

What sounds, what sympathy, what silence, what
Creation? What recompense? What word? What land?
What river bottoms once muscular, tracing lifelines,

Deltas, flood plains; what land bunching, ruffling,
What stones rolling, what wheels (wooden, steel,
Rubber), what riding out on horseback, what

Flick of wrist, tug of tether, blast of rock,
What melting of rubber, what extension of self, what
Squeak of progress, what eye, what level, what

Parcelling and flattening, what neatly bundling,
What legacy? What future? What expressway? What
Goat trail on steroids, what native path, canoe trail,

Wagon train, trail of tears, what aggregate composition,
What filleted history, what strata, what subplates,
What tectonic metaphor, what recoil, what never

Having to deal with the revulsion of self, only
The joy of forward, the joy of onward, the endless fuel:
The circles, the ramps, the fast lanes, the cloverleaf,

Perspective of elevation, the royalty of those views,
The Schuylkill, the Hudson, the Niagara, the skylines,
The people in their houses, passing women, men

Dressing, men unearthing, smoke pluming, what
Future? What the apple tree remembered? Not
Even the sound of fruit. If a body is no longer a body,

Where is memory? If a text is no longer a text,
Where is body? If a city is no longer a city, what road?
If future no longer has future, where does it look?

She snaps her cellphone closed: no one. Alone.
The century is elsewhere. She turns her back,
Swallows her words. She will do anything for home.

A MEMORABLE FANCY

At the toll booth she stopped to ask who was in charge of the expressway, or future, the words slipping back and forth in front of her. A large-headed woman, her hair roped and lashed about her head, looked up and held out her hand: *George Washington. Seven times.*

I have no money, she said, suddenly aware that this was indeed a fact, as was the yoke around the woman's upright neck. Her nostrils flared, her body strained against it, Al Green in the background. *Are you a poet?* she asked, meaning do you feel that tug? *The roar of tires is the rhythm of my day*, the woman said, *every fourteen cars a sonnet.* Behind her the city slickened: vehicles everywhere, idling, honking, revving, stiffening themselves against her. The braided woman did not flinch. *George Washington, seven times.*

I am lost, she said. *Can you tell me where to start?*

The braided woman's thumbs smoothed the air. *You can try Port Authority. But I wouldn't hold my breath.*

In response to the woman's kindness, she shared her latest vision: Louis XVI is alive and living in Washington, a staggeringly blind man filling his frame with BBQ ribs and glazed ham. Under his bed he keeps a rifle, thinking a cattle rustler might show up in the night. Deeply suspicious of his dreams

he hires a young woman to stand in the corner and lash
herself all night as he sleeps.

It doesn't matter if I see her, he said, *it's knowing she is somewhere
lashing herself.*

I I

THIS IS NOT MY BEAUTIFUL POEM

> 'It is crucial to see that ... the injured bodies would not be something on the road to the goal but would themselves *be the road* to the goal ... '
>
> Elaine Scarry

A: Once was income levels, measurements of perceived
    Noise levels, probability of pollutants, percentage
    Of truck traffic, thyroid levels and runoff acceptable, such

B: Levels! Much analysis of sentiment, surveys, no
    Lack of suitable data. Measure, position, men in overalls
    Smoking, pavement uneven, concrete dividers zipping

A: And unzipping lanes.

B: Free to move on: those who
    Find noise levels unacceptable. Home interviews, men
    Squirrels consulted. Index for design of mean maximums:

A: Those who live within 1,200 feet of the expressway

B: Those without the waterfront view,
    Those who thought that vehicular vistas had precedence
    Over the pedestrian, those who having decided modernity
    Was the new god, mobility its blood, those who understand
    Transactions to be the new gold: the exchange itself

A: Gold.
    Who can resist the smooth views from the Gardiner,
    The BQE, the Westside Highway, who can resist the thruway,
    Its momentum from the Great Lakes to the Atlantic,
        emptying itself?
    A momentum so forceful water rises forty storeys without
        a pump.

A: Who can resist
    The slide of modernity, of being elsewhere always, ahead of
    Oneself, texting oneself – not to bring modernity into
        the poem,

Pristine modernity, the dream – but modernity leaks, modernity

B: Is uncontainable, because transnationalism presents no barriers

To the acquisition of self, lease of self, layaway-plan self, because

Every transaction, even the most minute, considers

The implications of transactions, we don't care for smooth rides,

We care for opportunities to charge, you see? Liberty is

A: Defence of fees. The ability to charge a fee, liberty is worth

B: Charging for (we all agree) and every breath a logical measure,

Small gates inside our veins that open and shut, never

Mind thinking, never mind how the self will be outside

A & B: Of body and measured, as the roads are measured, as

The air is measured, as every resource is measured.

A: This poem stinks of dynamite.

B: There are ideas here you may not like.

A: Things have already been ingested.

B: Long ago, the fine print, like talcum powder.

A: Long ago you already said yes.

B: Long ago a deal was struck, something about pebbles and the weave of blankets.

A: Certain matters have been undertaken on your behalf.

B: Prior to this you had no experience.

A: Let sleeping cars lie, she said. Let little dogs go.

B: Now that you are accustomed to signing the waiver
   without reading.

A: Now that you are willing to say yes.

B: Now that you are willing.

A & B: Occupants must refrain from leaving the vehicle.

This vehicle believes it is a bigger vehicle.

If this vehicle is driving erratically let us know!

Without trucks America Stops.

Caution wide right turns.

Caution roadways congested: overpasses falling.

We hire safe drivers.

We deliver new solutions.

Schneider 30015 Flexi-Van Express.

Be a hero! Designate a driver.

How's my driving?

Do you need a driver?

If you see something, say something.

1-800-MyRights!

1-800-Freedom.

1-800-Express.

B: It's the order of things that keeps her up at night.

A: *This is not a poem*, she asserts with much exclamation.

B: She now suggests, pointing
   Outward, herself pointing
   A finger juts now
   Becoming a system of pointing

A: (No, not a system of owning)

B: Everyone is always upholding
   A system of containing that is concrete

A: (No, not a vessel overflowing)

B: Her finger, pointing, exits
The idea of everything
Fitting neatly

A: On your road, or expressway

B: (No, it is not *your* moon)

A: (No, I am not *your* begonia)
(No, there is no end to this)

B: His road would not hold
His road hung
made exits and entries
Almost unbearable

A: His road and how he made it
and all it contained
and no room for others
the smell of it lingering

B: His road never could reach
His road the most interesting thing not seen
His road unreachable

A: its miraculous order
all it maintained

B: His road where the undertow never reaches
His road above my head twisted

A: all of his blood
nailed and nailed

B: His road transubstantiation
His road on bricks
mortar
His road the aggregate composition of it

all that he did not leave

or

B: Seventeen pylons in the parking lot
Needing order
Now sixteen because it is even, and

A: Random

B: Several inches of brick
Several inches with three gashes
Several inches protruding
Several inches that want inclusion
Several inches gashing and protruding
Several inches without counting
Several inches solid

A: And random

A & B: Beautiful, beautiful the road stretching, birdlike, yawning from its nest, not all caught up in itself, not googling itself admiringly, just being its daily self, how we all ride its coattails. The road stretching, humid and damp, bringing no good news but itself passing, a shadow over us, under us, the road stretching ambulances and sparrow song, arterial to Atlantic and Flatbush, past Magic Johnson's Savings and Loan, its yarmulked peak and promise of luxury condos, beautiful, beautiful, the dying pansies and the face of noon, the tightening at the back of the knee, the road reaching.

B: There is nothing between me and my poems.

A: There is nowhere between you and your expressway.

B: Fleeting, fleeting, the backs of your heels, the salt on my tongue.

A & B: Beautiful, how the road arched, there, the lift of it, the off-ramp, beautiful toll, the elbow, beautiful the straight stretch, the bridge, the straining overpass, the roiling Gowanus, the brick of Cobble Hill, the pools of light, the angry women outside their cars, yelling something harsh when I press my thumb to the back of your leg (this has no business here, but it remains).

No business.

Remain.

A MEMORABLE FANCY

She lifts the expressway's veil. Hardly modest but, still, a crevice here and there to slip into. Skin is removable, she tells herself, it's not surprising.

A man stands, cradling his elbows. His face, an elephant's behind with eyes, and a mouth that seems uncertain of its origins, mouth that is not self and no less confident for the mystery. When she approaches he barely moves, and when he speaks neither does his mouth. *It's not my century*, he says, *nor the one you imagine. Time is not as tame as you believe, and intention not as pliant, not as neutral. We move, we consume, we respond, we spew; one man's garbage is another man's narrative ... you won't arrive anywhere.*

How do you know what I want? she asks, stepping over empty things multiplying underfoot.

No way out for humans. No way above, no perspective, no end to suffering, no such, none such. Not imagination enough. Nor vision enough, nor will to see what is to be seen, hear what is to be heard, write what is to be written.

But surely one human is not all humans?

Oh yes, separate the air from air, the sea from sea, sky from sky, quadrants, yes, make visible, no? Learn forget, learn forget. Make useful humans. Ah. What to do, what to do? Doesn't want to feel bad, human. Doesn't want to suffer. But the sheer number of things in piles, on barges, shipped out to sea, tiny things, once used, a matter of great inconvenience ... found here, you'll agree, not a comfortable place, not a largeness of spirit. Crevices. Tiny orifices, forgotten, long ago, forgotten, never to be patched up ...

And you? You have your ear, no? You have your ear on the nape of time, the downspout, pure, rollicking, endless, without direction, heavy, heavy, and dense.

Is there something I am supposed to take from this, she asks, *something to guide me?*

Ill-gotten gains, words. Loss. Dig hard enough, fast enough, you'll find meaning. Though I don't expect you will do, nor that you have any. Spine that is. Or will. And words suck back on themselves: dig as fast as you can, they roil and fill in. Roil and fill. A great sand, the mind, a pit falling in on itself.

And that? No, that won't be what you thought, or where. Never is. Never was, and all of that, even he, you know the great word-pirate, even he fell short, and he the visionary, and he the wanderer, and he ... well, by now you may get my meaning.

It's been done before?

Yes. Though perhaps not by better.

III

BECAUSE EVERY ROAD IS MADE
WITH DYNAMITE

> 'I came back to the meadow. I could not shake
> the memory of a train.'
>
> Elizabeth Willis

ENDLESS INTER-STATES

1

They go down to the expressways, baskets
In hand, they go down with rakes, shovels
And watering cans, they go down to pick

Beans and trim tomato plants, they go down
In wide-brimmed hats and boots, passing
By the glass-pickers, the Geiger counters, those

Guarding the toxic wastes. They go down
Remembering the glide of automobiles, the
Swelter of children in back seats, pinching, twitching,

Sand in their bathing suits, two-fours of Molson's
In the trunk of the car. They go down, past
The sifters, the tunnellers, those who transport

Soil from deep in the earth, and are content
To have the day before them, are content to imagine
Futures they will inhabit, beautiful futures

Filled with unimagined species, new varieties of
Plant life, sustainable abundance,
An idea of sufficient that is global. Or,

Because cars now move on rails underground,
The elevated roads are covered in earth,
Vines drape around belts of green, snake

Through cities, overgrown and teeming
With grackles and rats' nests, a wall
Of our own devising, and the night

Watchmen with their machine guns
Keeping humans, the intoxicated,
Out. I am sorry for this vision, offer

You coffee, hot while there is still
Coffee this far north, while there is still news
To wake up to, and seasons

Vaguely reminiscent of seasons.

2

Web-toed she walks into the land, fins
Carving out river bottoms, each hesitation
A lakebed, each mid-afternoon nap, a plateau,

Quaint, at least that is my dream of her,
Big shouldered, out there daydreaming
The world into existence, pleasuring herself

With lines and pauses. How else? What is a lake
But a pause? People circling it with structures, dipping
In their poles? Once she thought she could pass by

Harmless. Scraping wet shale, her knees down in it, she
Tries to remember earth, that ground cover. She tries
To reattach things, but why? What if the world

Is all action? What if thought isn't glue, but tearing?
She sits at the lake edge where the water never meets
Earth, never touches, not really, is always pulling

Itself on to the next.

3

Now she sits by her memory of meadow, forlorn, shoeless.
She could scoop PCBs from the Hudson, she is
Always picking up after someone. But what? What

Is the primary trope of this romp? Where her uterus
Was the smell of buckshot and tar, an old man chasing
Her with a shotgun across his range. Cow pies and

Hornets' nests, gangly boys shooting cats with BB guns,
Boys summering from Calgary, trees hollowed out,
Hiding all manner of contraband goods. When she peers

In the knotted oak, classic movies run on
The hour, Scout on the dark bark, Mildred
Pierce with a squirrel tale wrap. Nature is over,

She concludes. Nature is what is caught, cellular,
Celluloid. She sticks a thumb in another tree, a
Brownstone, a small girl – her heart a thing locked.

It's been so long since she felt hopeful. (Perhaps nature
Is childhood.) The morning after Chernobyl
Out there with tiny umbrellas. All those internal

Combustions. This is a country that has accepted death
As an industry, it is not news. She has been warned.
Her ratings sag. She scans her least apocalyptic

Self and sees mariners floating, Ben
Franklin penning daily axioms, glasses lifting
From the river bank, planked skirts on Front,

China-like through the industrious, thinking, traffic
Clogged city, its brick heavy with desire for good.
Memory of meadow, Dickinson an ice pick scratching

Wings in her brain: if you see her standing, if you move
Too quickly, if you locate the centre, if you have other
Opportunities, by all means if you have other opportunities.

4

Abandoned mine shafts on either side, those
Tight curves between Kaslo and New Denver,
Hairpin at glacial creek, splash of red

Bellies muscling, streaming up, we see them
From the open window. Or once did. Even here?
Salmon stocks diminish, mammals dying off.

No, he said, not in your lifetime. Vertical;
Traces where the charge went off,
Ruggedness is your only defence, he

Said, be difficult to cultivate, navigate. Offer
No hint of paradise, no whiff of
Golf course. Uninhabitability your only

Recourse. Lashed, that moment, prolonged
Leaving, her father on the roadside
Dreaming his world fitting in some place,

Without being reigned in, her father's fathers
Throwing rocks down on Hannibal,
Straddling the last large elm in the valley,

Knowing where and how to lay the charge, or
Sucking shrapnel from an open wound,
The lambs all around, bleating.

5

Which lifetime? Beyond what brawn? Who
Knew where the road would take us?
Neat, neat, the rows of apple trees

There in the valley, red summers, the heat
Of Quebecois pickers, vws in a circle,
Firepit and strum. Men from Thetford

Mines dreaming peaches, dreaming
Clean soil. Hour upon hour the self
Becomes less aware of the self.

Beautiful, beautiful, the centre line, the road,
This power station and control tower, these
Weigh scales, these curves, that mountain

Goat, those cut lines, these rail lines, that
Canyon, the Fraser, the Thompson,
The old highways hyphenating

Sagebrush, dead-ending on chain
Link, old cars collecting like bugs
On the roadside, overturned, curled, astute,

Memory of the Overlanders,
Optimism, headlong into
Hell's Gate. Churn of now,

The sound barriers, the steering
Wheel, the gas pedal, the gearshift,
The dice dangling, fuzzy,

Teal, dual ashtrays, AM radio
Tuned to CBC, no draft, six cylinders,
The gas tank, the gearshift, easing

Into the sweet spot behind
The semi, flying through Roger's
Pass; the snowplow, the Park

Pass, sun on mud flap, the rest stop
Rock slides, glint of snow, the runaway
Lanes, the grades steep as skyscrapers,

The road cutting through cities,
Slicing towns, dividing parks,
The road over lakes, under rivers,

The road right through a redwood,
Driving on top of cities, all eyes
On the DVD screen,

All minds on the cellphone,
The safari not around, but inside
Us: that which fuels.

6

No matter, the slither of pavement is endless,
Today the rain, a gold standard, all the
Earmarks of, never mind, all is well, all

Is well, and who doesn't want to hear that?
She gets on her scooter and roars, she gets
On her skateboard and feels the air under

Foot, she shakes out her hair, thinking of California,
Thinking of allergies, thinking of the wreck
Of place: who ever promised more? The iris

With its feigned restraint, the daring tuba,
The horn of shoe, utilitarian, delicate. Such
Useful domesticity, such hopeful electronics.

Once she disappeared by turning sideways.
Now she finds it difficult to reappear. She lifts
The sediment of time to her palm, feels it sift

Between her fingers: bone, bits of event. Aren't
We all a bit fluish this century? Nothing bearing any
Mark of otherwise. No prescript, nothing a bit of hope

Won't cure. Such a churn of optimism:
That which consecrates will not kill. Maybe New York?
She fits herself on an easterly course: been done,

Been done, but what better than the well-trodden
Path? Beautiful, beautiful, the seams
Of the rich, their folded linens,

Their soft bags of money. If it ain't broke
Don't fix, if it ain't resistant, don't
Wince, if it fits like a boot, then boot it.

And so she does.

A MEMORABLE FANCY

A voice came to her through the din of traffic and commuter trains. Who are you? She stopped, her feet sinking into marsh. She had heard that question before and was prepared this time. *I am a person who pays bills*, she yelled. *I am a person who responds! I am a good person: I go along without much trouble.*

Why is complacency good?

A shimmer of scrap metal caught her eye. She squinted and considered its origins. Did understanding matter? All those bodies being shuffled to the furnace. All those acres of rain, forest, all those rivers, frogs, pigs, feathers. All those skins being shed … all those containers. The partitions, the tags, the inevitability of embodiment. A voice chastised her for thinking so darkly. *You are what you think*, it said, *and you think very dark thoughts.*

I am seeing, she yelled. *I am tired of the tyranny of the optimistic! I want a revolution of the optimist! I want a sincerity that sees!*

The voice carried on into the night. What blindness had she suffered? What deafness? She felt the pain of the world moving through her, lengthening her limbs, restarting her heart; expanding her veins until she felt she could explode. Cells like engines. Skin like a touch pad. Her body lashed. It was painful to think of movement. She held her translucent hand up to the sun and tiny poems revealed themselves to her.

They were of no use, but they pleased her nonetheless. Is that what it all means?

I am seeing, she said again at dawn, her feet squelching. *Can you hear me?*

Yes, I hear you, but you delude yourself if you think you see anything other than what you choose to see.

So do you! she yelled, imagining many faces there in the sunrise.

Perhaps. But knowing that, I don't inflict myself on others.

IV

CRASH

'What a mess with a lot of traffic in view in Brooklyn with the WINS Jam Cam. The eastbound side of the BQE very slow coming up from just past the Battery Tunnel split, past the Brooklyn Bridge and on into, uh, well, it looks like a lot of people are choosing the Manhattan Bridge.'

Kenneth Goldsmith

CRASH

A 58-year-old woman from San Jose. Three-car crash turns deadly. Multiple-car crash along the Atlantic City Expressway. Gas station in shambles overnight. SKOKIE car crash kills passenger on Edens Expressway. 'It then veered to the right across four lanes of traffic and overturned in the right grassy area. Two car crashes briefly. The Beachline Expressway is open this morning. Woman dies in expressway car crash. Crash test: David Cronenberg's most controversial film. 'A driver picked me up around midnight under the Gardiner Expressway.' The car crash may be one of Hollywood's most rudimentary clichés. San Jose woman dies in car crash on Capitol Expressway. Author David Halberstam killed in crash near Dumbarton Bridge, at the intersection of Bayfront Expressway and Willow Road when his car was broadsided. Multi-car crash on Expressway injures one. Thunder Bay News: One woman is in hospital as investigators continue to piece together. *Cached. Similar pages. Note this.* Ronald Wright, 65, was killed Wednesday in a six-car crash in Surprise, Arizona. Police kept the expressway shut down for hours. The expressway remained open at 1 p.m., with traffic moving slowly. Girl dies, family hurt in car crash. Expressway traffic disrupted between Iyo-Komatsu and Kawauchi, according to police car crashes head-on with tanker. It's an expressway, not a street! It's a lot harder to cross the central line of an expressway. Multiple-car crash caused tunnel to be closed and disrupted traffic on Honam Expressway. *Cached. Similar pages. Note this.* Three suffer critical, serious injuries after multiple car crash. Reckless driver on the BeachLine Expressway this morning caused chain reaction. The amount of car crashes goes up every month. CONCHESTER HIGHWAY, PENNSYLVANIA; COMBS MOUNTAIN PARKWAY, KENTUCKY; SCHUYLKILL EXPRESSWAY, PENNSYLVANIA. Jawa Report: Car Crash Leads To FBI Terrorism Task Force Investigation. Multi-vehicle crash on the Stevenson Expressway. Connect with Kids: Girls & Car Crashes. Online Dangers Part I: Posting Personal Info or son in the car, different driving situations, expressway, city streets. *Cached. Similar pages. Note this.* Halberstam's driver speaks. When Jones' car was involved. A Menlo Park Expressway driver.

Halberstam's last conversation. Before a fatal,

just before a fatal.

When Jones' car was involved.

Real-life story about driving. I'm posting here a story of a guy who survived. Serious car crash. Once on the main road. Expressway is about 100 yards or so. Crash was reported shortly after 10:30 a.m. on the westbound Bayfront Expressway at Willow Road. According to the crash.

Heavy rainfall contributes to hydroplaning car crashes. Serious injury Friday when their car skidded off Interstate 44, knocked down an expressway sign. Bad Car Pile-Up Video. Amazing Footage of a Thruway Car Crash. Van Stalls in the Fast Lane on a Busy Expressway and Cars crash into it One at a Time. One person dies in multi-car crash near Dumbarton Bridge. Minor injuries but big delays after AC

Expressway accident. A woman who died in a car crash on Route 287 in Bridgewater has been identified as ... Jon Corzine's car crash and the injuries he suffered after failing to. The crash, mistakenly thinking it happened. The Expressway rather than the odd joker. An expressway is literally an expressway.

Nowhere is the expressway's fault. If your car crashes into me, it's your fault. Car crash collision and insurance stories. *Some stoopid wer-man putting her mascara on.* My father had a car crash once. Dodi Fayed narrowed by France. British officials announce impending formal inquiry into Paris car crash. Investigators say Henri Paul, who also died in crash on Paris expressway. French prosecutor reports body of driver in car crash that killed Princess Di. Early on October 8, 2004, a horrendous series of car crashes occurred on the expressway heading for Beijing, near the interchange with the Jinji Expressway. The Jingshi Expressway gets its name by the combination of two one ... A 58-year-old woman from San Jose is dead following a two-car accident. *Cached. Similar pages. Note this.* The cost of litigating an automobile accident claim against an insurance company. Car crash on the Oregon Expressway viewed 341 times. Involving two cars on Chicago's Eisenhower Expressway left one man dead. Just before.
Continue reading. Crash reported.
The driver of the car carrying Lawyer
blames student, bridging or interchanges.
When they widened this 'expressway'
(Lanes going east, lanes going west.)
In a recent car crash Just Off Spaghetti Junction.

Car Crashes into Petrol Station Making a left-hand.

His car was broadsided.

Fatal car crash in Al Ghusais. Police investigate.

Survivor remembers. Impact. Crash.

Plane crash-landed on a major expressway.

'Honeybee' dies in Two-car accident.

                Near Mustang Road.

Does this scene look familiar?

Though disappointed that they were beaten to the car crash
on the expressway, they suspect they will have another shot
at one before the night is over

Motor vehicle crashes are the leading cause of death among
Americans under the

        zones and railway crossings cause or contribute.

Crash traces the escalating fetishization of car crashes.

We were shooting along the expressway.

        traffic jamming

        State Trooper Injured

        convert the elevated expressway

veered off the West Shore

police chase ended in a car crash

        two innocent bystanders

reduce head excursion and the likelihood of injury in a crash

Generally speaking, China expressway development is still in
backwardness

Rank Vehicles By Dimensions/Capacities

New Car Crash Damage Withstand 60-mph car crashes

Sports legend killed Monday
Nine-vehicle crash stalls Expressway
A car heading east lost control
Sombre in wake of car crash
Evening of car crash performance art

Just hours after two sisters
Fiery, four-car crash on the Virginia Beach–Norfolk Expressway

England cricketer Ben Hollioake
in Perth the Porsche
          came off a ramp on an expressway
                    south of the city police chase ended in a car crash

                                        critically injured
                              two innocent bystanders
teen awarded $3.3 million for severe head injuries heading
west on Horace Harding Parkway, the service road of the
Long Island Expressway, at about 9 p.m.
    crashed into the pole at 188th. Tenacious reporting raised
early high-speed car chases, crashes, mystery,
    most importantly, a driver who witnessed the crash saw a
police car parked on the shoulder about a mile down the
expressway.

More trips on the Gowanus Expressway means more car trips
on the local streets. Corridor auto use on air pollution, crash
deaths and injuries accidents, 2 nites ago a 15 years old kid
died on the spot in a car crash in hometown, his parents were

in the other car. The expressway dispatcher spoke of hearing about 150 Cars Involved in Chain Crash on U.S. Highway. Two people

killed

    dozens injured

        Friday in a chain car crash involving as many as 150. Tow truck blows tire, car crash on the Brooklyn-bound upper level of the Verrazano-Narrows involved in a fatal car crash. *If you've been seriously injured in a car crash, or have lost a loved one* … 'Analysis of the Dynamics of Automobile Passenger Restraint Systems.' Andy Warhol, Green Car Crash, 1963 History Crash Course. We want to bring an even higher level of satisfaction to Expressway Lube! Last year more than 150 teens died in Colorado car crashes. Drunk ran home after Bronx car crash, say cops. *Cached. Similar pages. Note this.* You're Good to Go.

V

SOME MOMENTS FROM A LAND
BEFORE THE EXPRESSWAY

> 'Lured by a little winding path,
> Quickly I left the publick road.'
>
> Dorothy Wordsworth

LINES WRITTEN MANY MILES FROM GRASMERE

Grasmere, May–December 1800

1

Wm and John set off into Yorkshire
Cold pork in their pockets.
I could hardly speak when I gave

Wm a farewell kiss. Walked

As long as I could amongst the stones,
Wood rich, palish thick, and resolved
To write a journal of the time till

Wm and J. return. My resolve shall

Give Wm pleasure when he comes …
That I had a letter from Wm! Came on
Just when I was going, went forward

Much amused by stepping-stones.

Sauntered a little
Melancholy in my
Back.

2

In the evening round the lake
Up into the Black Quarter
The ashes still, lain out

A long time among the rocks.

On gathered mosses
To Ambleside
As far as Windermere thrushes

Not forgetting the Stone chats.

3

No letters! No papers!
Put by the linen, down Batchelor's
Buttons, mended in the morning

To Ambleside and found a letter

From Wm. On the other side of the lakes
To the foot of, towards Rydale, at
my favourite field, from, did not

Further.

Up to the rocks above Jenny Dockeray's
Left the water at near nine
In the morning to … resolving to go again

In evening. One from Wm and 2 papers.

To the Blind man's for plants: Strawberries
To the Potters, upon the hill, went bleating
In the road after tea, round the lakes after tea

Crossed the stepping-stones

Down rambling by the lake
Towards Mrs. Simpson's
No letter, no, and

A letter from Richard to John.

4

To lakeside in the morning
To the waterfall
On the hill above the house,

gathered wild Thyme with my 'load.'

Again upon the hill, more plants
To the Blind man's
As far as the Blacksmith's

By Loughrigg
No Wm!
I slackened my pace.

5

Up to Mr. Simpson's
Up the hill to gather sods
Down to the lakeside and took up orchises

The expectation of

And it was Wm! After our first joy,
The birds were singing, looked fresh,
Though not gay.

Afraid of the tooth-ache for

Wm cut down the winter cherry
stuck peas
unruffled like green islands

to Ambleside.

Chiding children, driving little asses
Hung in wantonness.
Wm went first alone

upon the water to set pike floats.

6

A fine morning and sauntering
Rain and warmer, tea and cold
Air the vale of little Langdale:

Wm caught a pike, 4 and ¾ pounds.

7

To Ambleside, to Rydale, to Loughrigg,
To Mary Point, to Wytheburn, to Keswick,
To Windy Brow, to Silver Hill, through Rydale
Woods, in Borrowdale, to Stickel Tarn,
To Langdale, to Mr. Olliff's gate

Wm writing his *Preface*.

To Borricks, to Ulswater and Churnmilk force,
At Fleming's, to Grisedale Tarn, the Michaelmas
Daisy droops

Wm still unwell.

8

A fine clear, warm sunny, sweet mild,
Supped and nailed, very pleasant yellow
Leaves and noise of boys in the rocks

Both Wm and Coleridge better.

Grasmere, October 1801 – February 1802

9

Coleridge Keswick Sara Simpson we day
Dined at Mr. Luff's, Wm and laudanum,
Coleridge and rain,

Misty and no further.

Rainy, wind, very fine, sweet sheep-
Fold, sea, miss, omitted.
To be anxious for him.

O

Followed Wm the rag boxes (up) hill,
The lake, tea and sky, dullish damp
And cloudy, anxious morning broth

To Churnmilk Force upon Heifer crags.

A very dankish, misty, wettish,
Dullish rainyish.
A fine frosty, keen frost, fine sunny

My heart smote

Melancholy and ill bowels.
Ay. We carried the Boxes cross
The Road to Fletcher's peat house.

Yellowish-green after tea.

Fine soft gleams of sunshine, thin
Fog ascended the lucky wind a sharp
Hail shower gathered at the head

Impressed we melted into sonnets.

10

Wm raked a few stones off the garden,
I cut shrubs. Moveless clouds, soft
Grave purple on the waters, stupefied,
Spread out like a peacock's tail.

Molly washing. Read Smollett. Snell
In Wanly Pension. Misbound Chaucer
But a leaf or two affecting letters: Coleridge

Resolved to try another Climate.

Read to fetch in Lessing and Grammar
A Chaise came past, we sent off
Toward letters, stopped at Park's

For straw in Wm's shoes.

Pedlars by a bright wood fire
Countenances rosy in crossing,
Lantern out at the Tarn

All perished: cloaks drying at

The public house the day before
Their funeral. Little peat fire grew
Less and starved 'a star or two beside.'

Snow altering and refitting the Pedlar,

A present of eggs, mountains palish,
Buffish, roads melted snow, but
I concluded, a safe passage over Kirkstone.

Grasmere, February–May 1802

11

Carman cheering horses, wildness
Of a Mountain lass but a Road lass
Traveller from Birth who wanted

Fresh blown fagging up the steepness.

A miserable clashy snowy foggy very
Rainy wet misty grey frosty-sunny
Excessive simplicity calm and rich:

Slashing away in Benson's wood.

Made of my shoulder a pillow and read
My Beloved slept, a poem in bed
Singing fire and owls: a sailor begged

to Glasgow in a sweet tone.

12

Wm sitting on stones
Feasting in silence, lingered
Long looking down under

Common ash yew ivy holly

In rows, a sweet moss
Carpet: resolved to plant
Having copied the Prioress's

Tale. He with his eyes shut

No one waterfall
Above another
Waters: the voice

Of air. Ridges

The backs of sheep owing
To their situation; we
Spread a fur gown then

Came the lake slipping.

   Grasmere, May 1802 – January 1803

13

On the Rays a woman half-
Starved 2 girls a pair of slippers
Had belonged to some gentleman's

Child – not easy to keep on

Too young for such travels
Husband gone off with another,
And she *pursued*: fury, tears

Moved, I gave her a shilling.

14

Sunshiny coldish hackberry crab
Blossom, anemone nemorosa, marsh
Marigold speedwell, beautiful blue

Butterflies and Wm asleep

In the window, his chest, the hills hoary,
A winter look; God stripping the trees,
Forms I skimmed, what freedom storms.

Wm haunted with altering the Rainbow.

Swallows come to the sitting-room
Twitter and bustle, hang, bellies
To the glass, forked fish-like tails

Swim round

And round again they come,
Wm (again) attempting to alter,
Then added a little Ode.

V I

THE ENDLESS HUM

'The American really loves nothing but his
automobile: not his wife his child nor his coun-
try nor even his bank-account first … but his
motorcar.'

William Faulkner

'Recently in the Peruvian Amazon a man asked
the writer Alex Shoumatoff, Isn't it true that the
whole population of the United States can be
fitted into their cars?'

Annie Dillard

PROGRESS

One is not simply.
One is not.
One is ever after.
One is as much as this.
One severs heads.
One appears in public for a fee.
One appears and later.
One becomes one.
One indeed.
One becomes one.
One is never many.
One is a sumptuous red bean bun.
One is coveted.
One is scrambled.
One must not hesitate to think.

And another thing!

Or this.

This, or this and this ...

The expressway was born in A.
What is more self-referential than A?
Either, or.
The thing goes round on itself, the thing goes round.

And no one ever dreamed it would stagger, would stumble, or
    no one
Ever dreamed.

What citizens of A lack in political options they make up
for in pastry choices, in supermarket items, in numbers, in
health-insurance packages, in phone plans, in ways to choose
because:
Freedom is to confuse.
Freedom is to make a buck.
Freedom is to charge a fee.
Information is available for those who can acquire it.
After all, this is A.
After all, freedom.
So, that is A.
Fees are A.
The expressway is A.
All along the strip malls fees are charged, or not. There is a
    choice.
Everyone has a choice.
Freedom has a choice.
Freedom is a commodity.
Freedom is not a commodity you need to own.
Freedom is a choice.
Freedom has conditions.
Freedom is exportable.
Freedom is a fee.
Freedom is available for import.
Freedom is as freedom does.

What does Freedom see when she closes her eyes?

I don't understand this option.
Or, I don't recognize this as an option.
Or, the option that I want is not offered.
Multiple choice offers no room for thinking, only choosing.
What if I do not like your poll?
Several options roving down the road.
Or, an option walked into a bar.
Or, what every cowgirl needs is a good option.
Or, citizenship becomes membership.
If anything is clear from the twentieth century it is that
    governments have failed.
If anything is clear from the twentieth century it is that
    corporations have won.
If anything is clear from the twentieth century it is that
    membership has rewards.
If anything is clear from the twentieth century it is that
    no one can afford to be loyal.
That the individual is all alone.

Health care is (not) an option.
Health care is (not) a commodity.
In A, lives are not commodities.
In A, the best minds are not commodities.
In A, what is said is not what is meant.
In A, everyone always says yes even if they have no intention.
In A, they don't need intention, or action, they need only to
    say yes.

In A, body parts.
In A, bodies.
Why not come to A?
Why not set up shop?

MURMURINGS, MOVEMENTS OR
FRINGE MANIFESTO

O little expressway, miracle of expressway, upended galaxy, extended Adirondack slither, downhill from Syracuse to Manhattan, glorious, glorious, no longer carrying but being us, us moving everywhere, all around the globe.

She asserts herself into the grain:
B: Writing is not a commodity
A: (Unless published).
B: Original is not a commodity
A: (Unless patented).
B: Writing is thinking made visible
A: (Unless it isn't).
B: Original is what you haven't seen
A: (What hasn't been reproduced).
B: Writing is a disordered hum
A: (What is disordered is useless to the market).
B: Original is singing
A: (Recognizable).
B: Writing is always forward
A: ( ).
B: Original is what you don't recognize
A: (What you don't recognize isn't there).
B: Writing is the space between this
A: (Original is overrated)
B: And this
A: (Is anomaly)

B: Space

A: (Who needs this?)

B: Is only in relation to stopping whereas
Language

A: (Only what is functioning)

B: Persists and
Original is ornery

A: (Of no value on its own).

B: Or, if somewhere in the suburbs?

A: ( )

B: This dynamite stinks of poem.

A: One morning thousands showed up and inch
By inch tore up the expressway and carried it off in their
beaks.

B: In another city they tore off their earmuffs, unplugged
The white-noise machines, hung up their car keys,
And took to the pavement in wonder.
In another city, frozen citizens dropped to their bellies
Like penguins sliding toward the Great Lakes.

A: The expressway is the future.
The expressway is the market.
The expressway is the line endless.
The expressway contains multitudes.
The expressway directs and projects.
The expressway with its chapel and truck stops,

B: Its whorehouses and science centres,
Its indiscriminate will to connect.

A: They are outside, moving things.

B: Under the sun, moving things.

A: On the horizon, moving things.

B: This one sweeping.

A: All across the land, men out on back steps looking.

B: When a man looks what does he see?
    When a man with his hardhat, when a man in boots.
    When a man reaches out his hand.
    When a man becomes a man.

A: When a woman becomes a man.
    When a woman looks at a man.
    When a woman in her hardhat, when a woman in boots.
    When a man sees a woman.

B: When the woman is not young.

A: is not yet old.

B: When the day is long.

A: is cool and longing.

B: When the woman is nowhere to be found.
    When the man with his stop sign.

A: When the cars, all of them surround us.

B: ( )

A: Thinking is not hostile.

B: She insists against the grain.

A: One or more of you will die. One in four, seven in ten,
    nine in ten, one in twenty, twelve in eighteen, fifty-fifty or
    roll the dice, luck of the draw, dice of the throw, tip of the
    cup, turn of the wheel, toll of the table, ace of spade,
    shovel of hearts, dig of luck, stroke of break, deuces wild,
    obtuse, obdurate, crazy as cousins, a statistic in kind, a
    hovering in lamb.

A & B: The poem refuses to start from a position of safety and end in a position of safety having momentarily revealed a tiny fracture in human existence, the equivalent of a fly (a very small one, possibly a fruit fly even) in the chardonnay, or perhaps even more revelatory, a dose of chemotherapy (but not yours), a glimpse into the abyss (a tiny one, twice removed) and back to the front porch (this could be yours), before the next sip, because the poem is a connector, the poem is not a country lane, there is nowhere that doesn't lead here, there is nowhere here cannot find there. Everywhere is capable of being here now. There is nowhere this is not. There is nowhere I.

A MEMORABLE FANCY

In the strange din of morning traffic she found herself outside a cottage half sunk in a scum-covered pond, next to an abandoned rail line, old power lines like fly rods casting. She knocked twice. A Poet opened the door and invited her in. *Lean this way*, the Poet said, which meant she leaned in the opposite way. The floor creaked, the walls slid. A turtle looked up from the sill, cocking its head like a lapdog.

I'm going to introduce you to my other, but if you're not more approachable you'll get nothing in return.

I want for nothing, she said, folding her arms tight.

You think you want for nothing, the Poet said.

A small opening appeared in a wall through which she saw a room exactly like the room they stood in. *Go through the little door.*

But I won't fit through the door.

Just walk.

And as she walked she shrunk and once through the door she expanded. The Other stood at a table pouring something out. She remembered to smile, as instructed, and approached slowly.

You're substantial, the Other nodded. *Thirsty?*

No, she thought, remembering the water of New Jersey, but she took the cup and sipped politely.

You think the expressway is the future, but you are wrong.

I am?

You think you can imagine the future, but you are wrong.

I am?

You think the future is a lapdog, but you are wrong.

I am?

In the morning, when you look out your window, what you are seeing will not be the future.

It won't?

It won't. And for that you should be extremely grateful.

VII

MISDIRECTIONS

'There is no path to the future, the path is the future.'

Man on a bus

ACCEPTABLE DISSOCIATIONS

1

Meanwhile the expressway's hum, it roars into
Her, the expressway cargo and tree-lined, stretched
Radio towers, mowers its horns and hogs, its beef

And bread vans, hour after hour, laptops, radar
Detectors from New Mexico, Idaho potatoes, HoHos
And Cheetos, all organic grain-fed, pieces of chicken,

Pieces of cow, slices of pig, kernels of corn, diced carrot,
All packaged meals, she of drums, her mile after mile
Of interchange escape into itself rest stop, progress

Is welcoming and bidding adieu, states drinking
Her progress, passing tolls, Motel 6 she hum as glass
And EconoLodge, passing itself traces of Ashland

And Peoria, Willingboro, Paterson, every inch of it grafted,
Numbered, planted, barriered, mowed, guardrailed,
O my citizen consumers, for the the, infinite,

Replaceable, scaling these walls of sound and motion,
Dipping in, expressing oneself, expressing oneself,
Expressing oneself.

2

Wonder warships at citizens in blue, the number
Lining the leaf, infinite expressways, and scaling
Blood, soil a Camden, shouting over water Sunday

Steel passing the in and sky noise, another abandoned
By of one to mills, at steel, above bone, gazing (euphoria,
Nostalgia!) citizens, up leaf, citizens, wonder! Infinite warships

Sunday and abandoned a shouting expressways, noise,
Across in blood, steel, lining passing bone, at gazing
Blue mills, scaling the water another number to in

The above soil by of steel up one and sky at the
Over Camden, citizens, euphoria nostalgia!
All along the avenue spronging, tent-like, their attitudes

Way ahead of them. My computer screen, waving. *Where
Is your horse?* she said, and there was nothing I could say.
What I want is generally tidy. What I get often can't dance.

Who wants a date who can't dance?
Who wants a line without rhythm?
Who wants a line without thought?

3

Occasionally there is anger. Occasionally she takes her one good foot and applies it to surfaces otherwise flat and safe, the expressway progressing itself through her, expressly.

(I live here because the country I once lived in is now a corporate washroom, where there were once gardens now oil refineries turn night into day and farmers into militiamen – you won't ever understand this, and your teeth gleam!)

Once again the feeling comes, like a sprong in the groin, an abundance of feeling that is sharp, almost hostile in its need to overtake. Several women in pink felt it coming. They turned, their pierced ears like arrows in her thigh.

Sprong, sarong. I ask you?

Over the course of several weeks developers wiped out all the trees in a town in A to avoid having them designated as essential sites after a rare woodpecker was found to be nesting in the town. Woodpeckers are not essential. Trees are not essential. Trees are ornamental. Humanity is ornamental. Prophet is everything.

This poem resembles urban sprawl. This poem resembles the freedom to charge a fee. The fee occurs in the gaps. It is an event. It is not without precedent. It is a moment in which you pay money. It is a tribute to freedom of choice.

Reality is a parking lot in Qatar. Reality is an airstrip in Malawi.

Meanwhile the expressway encloses, the expressway round and around the perimeters like wagon trains circling the bonfire, all of them, guns pointed, Busby Berkeley in the night sky.

DIVINING ROD, OR HOW TO FIND A NEURAL PATHWAY HOSPITAL EXIT: EMERGENCY LANE: HOV

1

This idea is chaos, landing gear
Stuck in the cold, the expressway below
Expressing. Three legs, tumultuous sleep.

Thank you, Durinder, lines across the border
Are moved by circumstance, here
It is money, only money that speaks. Not

The body on its last heaves, and a sister
Somewhere trying. She says goodbye
To the expressway, thankful of having moved

Through the blizzard toward her sister, her
Tenacity, her experience of exposure to DDT.
Cancer the longest relationship in her life.

But what are years now? Miles, ticking
Per litre, movement: the expressway,
Its millions of bodies hourly exiting

And entering, random the cell
With its division, millions hourly, dividing.
We rely on so much chance, why

Shouldn't our cells mutate? Holding up
A five-legged frog, a three-legged frog, where
Are the thirteen angles? Where the guardians,

Where, over the land, in the furrows, where
The stones that will rise and, with terrific force,
Hammer themselves home?

2

Pulling herself out of a slump at the word *metastasized*
(Liver like a torn lace tablecloth barely functioning), now
Men with orange hats and spades along the veins, resting.

Hospice, radiation, she spins the wheel, *No,*
Not this time. Randomize these options, offer up
Another route, surely there must be (detour?)

Something other than pain? I want to go home,
She says, but not this way, not these roads,
Not this buzz: *black milk of daybreak, I sing,*

All along the expressway, its terminal
Ambulances, those men sanding away the day-old
Growth, those men in combat boots, waving flags,

Saluting, directing traffic, rolling out the macadam
The way the body holds the road, the body with its
Neural pathways and depression like a layer

Of egg whites tightening the skin. Those men
With their backs against the road, with their backs
Against the sun, all day unravelling tar, hot

And swilling sweat in their strap boots, skin
Of roads and trucks with them, in them, heavy
Loads, the concrete cracking. *No to radiation,* she

Says, dreaming her hands at ten and two, heading
Down or away, the expressway transporting her out,
Out of the city and into valley beyond:

Men with spades digging. No one said ginger
Was a fruit, belonged here, ate several heart-
Shaped boxes of candy. Nothing to do with

Expressways, but she leaves it in for the sweeper,
Always a little something for the sweeper.

3

Lying on the examination table, her bowels
On the ultrasound in front of her, *There*, he says,
Pointing to the mass of toxins, *So, we inject*

This solution, its sole purpose to find
And surround the toxins, sealing them in,
Before they can do any more harm.

There are hard pebbles inside? *Yes, hard*
Pebbles, toxic, but entirely benign
Once they are sealed, and perhaps eventually

They will pass through us … And the sun,
The nurse behind the doctor says,
The sun will set and all around the world women

Will come out of their caves, lift up their burkas
And hold their wombs like compasses.

A MEMORABLE FANCY

By late morning she had stumbled into what appeared to be a wooded area: a vacant lot, an apparition, something forgotten, a place not visible from the rumbling train. She longed for something: perhaps a deer to nibble on the blackberry bushes and calm her nerves, or even blackberry bushes, or a deer, a bit of bark to rub her back against, earth to dig for grubs – suddenly she is hungry.

A man in the distance, on a rock, a fisherman in suit pants and suspenders, his white sleeves rolled up, about to wash his bowl for the New Year.

Is that water fresh?

When we were children we swam here not knowing what strange growths we were courting. But this clean bowl will not be eaten from, and that is often what I think of our future.

I have been walking toward the future, she says, *I want to meet it head on and, when I do, I want to know what to say.*

Once there was an appetite for such things. Now, we swill the future in our bowls not expecting anything to be clear. But we have life, no?

Is that enough? Isn't there someone who sees beyond all of this? There is someone in all of us.

Someone specific. Something specific. You with your bowl. That train. The dented skyline. Endless war. The future like a shard of glass. What can anyone say?

You can say, Calm. You can say, Slow. You can say, Enough. You can say, Easy. You can say, Pine, and mean it. You can say, Polish and breathe. You can use your tongue, and eye. You can check your pulse, let your hair grow, take less. You can suck on peaches. You can walk. You can read. You can let your mind wander. You can wonder. You can eat words. You can reach out. You can wait for clean, or you can make it so …

I am weary. I walk and walk and meanwhile the expressway hums …

What for weary? We all hum.

I am weary, I have so little hope.

Weary, maybe. But, no hope? For that there is never an appropriate time.

VIII

REST-STOP CULTURE OR
WAL-MART NATION

> 'And you may find yourself behind the wheel of
> a large automobile ... '
>
> David Byrne

THE ROAD IS EVERYWHERE EQUALLY

*You don't like this country you can move on down the road, that's
what you can do, just move on down the road ...*

Where is down the road? Where is away? Where is outside
Of market? Where does the road not lead? Where
Without cloverleafs? Where with unique air? What bubble?

How big a gate? Who gets in? What price tag? What
Automobile? Someone, somewhere, is having this precise
thought. Now. Or now. They are thinking it as they peel away

A bit of knee-scab. Remnants of a literary tumble.
Fringed skin. Or now tugging his hair on a train to Rangpur,
Sucking in his right cheek, thinking, *Why am I not original?*

Why am I not America?

Found on an off-ramp, her heels clicking.
Found under the overpass, tin can and methane.
Found with one shoe and a stump of coal.
Found a plastic can holder embedded around its neck.
Found forty-seven deer, seventeen domestic animals, one
     silver fox.
Found one thousand thirty-six water bottles.
Found fourteen hundred empty potato-chip bags.
Found three headless pigs.

Found seven crates of frogs stacked on the sidewalk, still
singing.
Caught masturbating while driving through Burger King.
Caught masturbating while driving through a car wash.
Caught having phone sex while driving.
Caught on a lane diversion without a licence.
Glad not to be driving though my head still thinks it is.
Caught with a K-car inside a tractor-trailer.
More asshole truckers taking over slow lanes.
Listen, Idiot Richard, I live in N.J., I have to pass air-pollution and
safety inspection every two years, so should you!
Man killed in a dispute over lane changes.
Found several lot lizards and two baby elephants.

Give me a car and a truck stop.
Give me a tank of gas.
Don't you love the smell of gasoline?
Seven syringes, infamous pancakes.

More fear than compassion, she found the monk out
On the expressway meditating, she found the monk breathing
Fire, she found him barefoot and restless, there, in the way

That we breathe, *Not about numbers, never,* he said, *that impulse*
To brand, to tattoo, to make accounts of what can not be counted:
All I have is this breath and even that is mingled with you.

What unnatural heroes we have made, while the real
Ones move the earth daily, blade by blade.

What to say in the face of whole paragraphs:
I agree, I agree, your wisdom like a gun to my head.

What to say in the face of unending pavement:
I agree, I agree, your wisdom like a gun to my head.

THE GREY HILLS OF OXFORD

Thirty-six-inch with several contusions, thirty-six-
Inch bald, slight wear on the right, thirty-six-inch
With a six-inch tear, thirty-six and evenly worded,
Thirty-six on its side, thirty-one with evenly spaced
Bald patches, larger with fist-sized treads, upright
With fist-sized treads, half-buried with the right side
Flattened, one rim with only a ripple of tread, two
Melded together, one mag wheel with a sliver
Of dark centre, three like links in a chain,
Three like leaking clay, one like a grey whale's
Snout, two flattened whitewalls on top of three
Barely discernible tube-like shapes, several earth
Tones near a white crumb of tire, seven stacked
Like folded commas, two very grey, burned tire
Corpses, something like a tractor tire, bigger
Than the others and basking in the sun, upper-
Most on the tire pile, near the canyon walls.

Four tires like forgotten bobsleds at the bottom,
Several tires jutting out from the earth,
Several at the top disentangled, but not free,
Sitting on the earth, half immersed.

At a distance, tires lose their particularity,
Tires become brushstrokes, hills
Fading into sky.

THREE DREAMS OF THE EXPRESSWAY

1 DISMANTLING

The men build and the women dismantle.
On this day the women appear one by one,
Despite our best theories, they drop their

Laptops and iPods, they leave their magazines,
They step down from elliptical trainers, out of
The boxing ring, tummies flat and minds sharp,

They move out of the domestic sphere, they
Move away from the office towers, they come
Down to the expressways with pickaxes, they come

With hammers, they come, suddenly clear,
Suddenly swinging hammers, they say, *This
Is a metaphor too unwieldy*, they say, *This*

Is a symbol that has undone us, they say,
This is the beginning of unmaking, they say,
The future is in doing the thing right, the future

Of the economy is in undoing, they say,
No more. You have come to the end of
The sound stage, they say, *You have hit a brick wall,*

They say, *The possible is now inside*, they say,
The new is reshaping the old, they say, *The new*
Plastic is the old infrastructures, they say, *Let the*

Planet for the planet be, they say,
They say, risking everything, they say, *Let the gaze*
Shift back to the probable, leave the untouched

Untouched, let the whales and elephants graze, the
Gaze turn inward, let the gaze turn in on itself.
And the women with their pickaxes unmaking.

Getting closer to the source of the friction, where
Tire meets pavement, his ear. *Is it the artists*
Who make song of the whirring with bumps and

Hollow manipulations of cars around figures?
Every invention a chance for whimsy. But how
To approach the silencing of roadways? *Look*

To the rubber, he says. A pattern in the tread?
A quality of aggregate? A speed? An engine?
A barrier? What will contain the vibrations? The 'snap'

Of the tire is what makes the noise: *Consider*
Melting vast quantities of tires stacked in
Landfills into liquid asphalt, consider a billion

Romance novels pulped, think of transformation
As surface, what we've read we now walk on,
What we've walked on we now live in, what

We've worn is now a sound barrier, and the cars
Silent as manatees.

3 RENEWAL

She goes down to the memory of river a slip beyond
The expressway. *This is not simply displacement*, she thinks,
Progress fuelled by hope. But trend is not destiny. Renewal

Is revision is opportunity for growth. She dreams women
On backhoes breaking up expressways, night and day,
Cracking the earth's concrete skin, earthquakes of relief

For the pinched and corseted. Women with sledgehammers
And picks, babies slung on their backs, not waiting
For the market to catch up with demand. Rerouting

Expressways, burying them, severing views: no cars
Tracing bodies of water, city avenues pedestrian, silent
Cars gliding past huge swaths of green, every rooftop

A garden, solar panels covering every parking lot, shading
And generating, outlets sockets, plugging into, the broad
Backs of old women out on concrete fields with hoes

At midnight with headlamps, peeling back, carting off
Whole sections of expressway to use as dams
Against the shifting tides. The expressway with

Its ethos of moving on, this town not good enough,
Get on the expressway. In this country
What I'm saying is another language,

In this country I could be deported.
In this country where the artists are busy unstapling
The seams. This country with its long lines, its speed

Bumps, its terrible blind spots, its weak knees, its history
Of war, its binaries, its tongue-tied, its revolution, its best
Intentions a noose around its own ankles, upended. Imagine

Texas with its future great wall and firing squads, its
Lone Ranger desire, six-shooter expressways in
And out of town, there is nowhere the expressway

Can't take or leave you, there is nowhere the expressway
Won't go, there is nothing it won't cover, nowhere
You can't hear it; nowhere you can't see it, but the shape,

The sound, the direction, those who ride, and how,
That is all to come.

A MEMORABLE FANCY

All along the expressway, gardens, and in them people. All along the expressway, trees, and in them birds. All along the expressway, rivers, and in them fish. All along the expressway, air, and in that, tires humming like baby birds.

Tell the people not to worry so much about their own gardens. Tell them to worry about the one garden.

She imagines the people out with wheelbarrows and spades, moving across the continent in waves, aerating the hardening crust. If you move out of your own garden? If your mind stays firm and wandering? If you listen? If you proceed?

Let no swath of concrete go without interruption, without puncture and connection.

Where do you go on a Sunday, when you are in need of rest? Make the earth that. Soothe, soothe.

They stand in waves. They hold their passports in the air.

IX

PROVERBS OF HELL

The body sublime, the heart SUV.

Fuel your plow with the blood of war.

Drive your car on the bones of the dead.

The road of CO_2s leads to rising seas.

He who is preoccupied with the afterlife pisses on the present.

So the price of oil goes, so goes the number of wars.

A fool sees product; a wise man sees shade.

He who sullies the earth sullies himself; he who dulls the sun
dulls his senses.

The future is the reversal of destruction.

Even a bee's too busy.

Profits are measured by the dollar, but real profit cannot be
measured.

A wholesome food comes in fewer than sixteen pieces from
seven states.

Prisons are built with the bricks of luxury items.

Let man wear the fell of the hemp seed, woman the fleece of
cotton.

The bird a thought, the spider a path, the mind the means.

What was once proved and known is now only rarely imagined.

What was once used to imagine now operates software.

The rat, the mouse, the starling, the squirrel; the lion, the
tyger, the elephant, the whale – only the useless, or root-
less, survive, otherwise: extinction porn.

The cistern pollutes; the fountain overflows, is of no use to
itself.

Once thought filled immensity; now it purchases goods.

To speak your mind is to be unpatriotic; to be human, then, is to be unpatriotic.

All things imagined must be images of truth; all things created must be fragments of our imagination.

The eagle never wreaked so much havoc as when he submitted to whims of profit.

The eagle provides for himself, but the air provides for the eagle.

Want in the morning. Buy at noon. Buy in the evening. Buy in your sleep.

He who has suffered you to impose on him knows the market.

As the plow follows markets, so the market follows itself.

The tygers of the market are no wilier than the corporate dogs.

Expect poison from the standing mind.

The coals of Wall Street, the bricks of despair, the last drop, the last grain.

As the cat chooses the warmest place to curl her bones so the wise man seeks home.

To create a new kind of flower is the splice of genes.

The best wine is the oldest, the best thought is the first.

Cheerfulness is the hammer of the right.

The expressway is a straight line, but the crooked road remains the road of genius.

Where man is, nature is bereft.

Where nature is not man, is not known.

Where nature is not natural, man is not man.

As a dog returns to his vomit, so a citizen to his belief in
    separation.
More is destruction.
Less is the wisdom of the future.
Abundance is all context.
The end of thought is the end of man is the end of earth.
In absentia, in absence, in obsolesce, or obnoxious.
Where nature is, man is not enough.
Enough, or too much. Too much.

Go forth and undo harm.

Go forth and do.

NOTES AND ACKNOWLEDGEMENTS

Notes on the text: 'Lines Written Many Miles From Grasmere' was crafted from the text of Dorothy Wordsworth's *Grasmere Journals*, Oxford University Press, 1971; 'Crash' was sculpted entirely from Google text. Quotes throughout the book are from, as follows: David Byrne, 'Once in a Lifetime,' *Remain in Light*, 1980; Annie Dillard, 'The Wreck of Time,' *For the Time Being*, New York: Knopf, 1999; William Faulkner, *Intruder in the Dust*, New York: Random House, 1972; Kenneth Goldsmith, *Traffic*, http://english.utah.edu/eclipse/projects/TRAFFIC/text.html, 2007; Elaine Scarry, *The Body in Pain*, New York: Oxford University Press, 1985; Wallace Stevens, *Wallace Stevens: Collected Poetry and Prose*, New York: Library of America, 1977: Elizabeth Willis, *Meteoric Flowers*, Middleton CT: Wesleyen, 2006.

Many of these poems have appeared in earlier versions in *The Common Review, Mipoesias, EOGH, The Malahat Review, The Capilano Review, Mantis,* and *Dandelion*. Thanks to the editors of each. Thanks to *belladonna, Poets House, The Poetry Project at St. Marks, and the Philadelphia poetry community for ongoing poetry dialogues. Thanks to all the Calgary folks, especially Janice Lee, Robert Majzels, Suzette Mayr, Christian Bök, derek beaulieu, the kids at the KP, and in memory of Rowland Smith. Finally, enormous thanks to Jackie Flanagan and the Markin Flanagan Writers Program for valuable time that led to the crafting of this work.

I want to thank Erín Moure for her ongoing ear and eyes. Thanks to Alana Wilcox (best eye ever), the entire Coach House team and Kevin Connolly for his generous reading. Bob, *bien sur*.

To my father, and all the road builders. And to those of us who watched it unroll.

Sina Queyras is the author of *Slip*, *Teethmarks* and *Lemon Hound*, which won the Lambda and the Pat Lowther awards for poetry, and the editor of *Open Field: 30 Contemporary Canadian Poets*. She currently lives in Montreal and keeps a blog, Lemon Hound.

Typeset in Charlotte and Charlotte Sans
Printed and bound at the Coach House on bpNichol Lane, 2009

Edited by Kevin Connolly
Designed by Alana Wilcox

Coach House Books
401 Huron Street on bpNichol Lane
Toronto, Ontario M5S 2G5

416 979 2217
800 367 6360

mail@chbooks.com
www.chbooks.com